G000161794

Rupert & Chutney McPhail's

Almanac of
Excuses

Lochar Publishing

© Chutney & Rupert McPhail, **1991**

Published by Lochar Publishing Ltd
Moffat DG10 **9ED**

British Library Cataloguing in Publication Data

McPhail, Rupert
      The almanac of excuses
      I. Title II. McPhail, Chutney
      828.91409

ISBN 0-948403-52-7

Printed in Great Britain by
Eagle Colourbooks Ltd, Blantyre, Glasgow

Acknowledgements

Our grateful thanks are due to the
following people:

Red Hector & Son for Illustration.
Jools for computing.
Patrick for organising things.

DEDICATION

To our dear mother
Brunhilde,
our sisters
Hiawatha and Lettuce
and our father
wherever he may be

(Daddy if you read this, please get
in touch with mother, who still
believes you were innocent)

CONTENTS

CONTENTS

Classification	Page

Getting away with it

When God confronted Adam in the Garden of Eden with the evidence that he had eaten the fruit of the forbidden tree, Adam's reply was factually correct; the Woman. Eve, had indeed given him the fruit and he had partaken of it. If we look more closely at the statement he gives however, we can see it for what it is - an excuse. Not the type of excuse calculated to get him off the hook altogether - Adam presumably knew that trying to fool God was unlikely to be a successful career move - but one based on what we can recognise today as the Diversion of Blame Technique, the idea being that in any set of circumstances, there is only so much blame going, and if you can get 20% of it going in someone elses's direction, well, that's at any rate 20% that's not coming in your own direction.

Eve, being only human, tried the same tactic, blaming the serpent for encouraging her in forbidden activity. The rest, as they say, is history. Although they are the oldest exponents of the excuse, our two ancestors are not really good examples to follow. Eve did show some promise in the art of lying her way out of a tight spot by blaming a non-human creature which, as a dumb animal, was a bit slow on the uptake & consequently unable to think of a thing to say: a trait shared by animals up to the present day, which explains their presence in so many of the great excuses of our time. But the biggest mistake made by both Adam and Eve was that they had but a very sketchy idea of the omniscience of the deity. In other words, they didn't know that God knew everything anyway, and that any excuses would thus be null and void.

This brings us to the first principle of the successful excuser - know who you're dealing with, because if you don't then you are liable to do yourself no little harm. If, for example, you explain your absence from work by saying that your car exhaust was blocked up by a hibernating Transylvanian whistling snail this may or may not be believed depending on the credibility of your employer. However, if the latter is a spare time breeder and noted expert in the habits of the Transylvanian whistling snail who knows that hibernation does not begin until the second week of next October, then you're in trouble. In other words, if you're going to lie, don't be found out through ignorance of your adversary.

As you will see, not all excuses work through the technique of Blame Diversion, as it is not always desirable or even possible to pull other people into the dock with you. It is probably true to say that large numbers of excuses work though the creative placing of a piece of doubt in the mind of the accuser as to whether you really deserve all the blame you were going to get for the set of circumstances which exist, or indeed, as to whether you are worth blaming at all! This "Smokescreen Technique" as it is termed, is a broad category ranging from the acceptable but timid "I'm late because I sprained my ankle coming up the stairs to the office", to the aggressive counter-accusation," When the hell are you going to get something done about installing a lift?."

The thing to remember about the Smokescreen Technique is that using it is a tricky balance between the banal and the preposterous, and this brings us to the second principle of the successful excuser - be careful how far you go. It's difficult to give an absolute rule for success here, other than by example. We would suggest that arriving late for work and explaining that the bus arrived late is not going far enough. It may well be true, but everyone's heard it, and it lacks the creative edge. On the other hand, arriving late and complaining bitterly to your boss about the meteor showers which damaged the Martian spacecraft thus delaying your return from Alpha Centauri is unlikely to be treated with much gravity (no pun intended) by your accuser. It will be assumed that you are joking, that you do not want the job after all, or that you have taken leave of your senses, none of which would be regarded by the connoisseur as a good outcome. You will have gone too far.

This second principle of excuses must of course be combined with the first. If you know your adversary well, and have irrefutable evidence that he or she is a fruitcake, the Alpha Centauri story, for example, may well be worth trying. It is this intuitive element which makes the success-ful use of excuses an art rather than a science. This theorising is all very well you ask, but does it work? Well, there have been legal cases where a charge of murder has been lessened because two accomplices each blamed the other and there was no evidence other than their own testimony to suggest who the true culprit was!

In more personal circumstances it's impossible to give an absolute guarantee. Once an excuse is given it can hardly be taken back, with a view to 'doing' the situation over again for purposes of empirical research. No-one is in a position to say what might have been. But would you take the risk of not having an excuse ready for immediate use?

"Immediate" is an important point here. The successful excuser is quick. So quick in fact, that the excuse is often there before the original accusation has been properly formulated. A good excuse, or even an aggressive counter-accusation will confuse matters, & if delivered with a degree of skill, is likely to leave the accuser wondering what the devil to say. Next thing you know, you've gotten away with it.

Think of the hot flush of panic which would come over you as the girl on the beach whom you've been examining through your telescope nudges her friend and points directly at you lens. If you get up and run there may well be a recognisable description of you in the evening paper. So you can't run. You'd better have an excuse ready.

Think of the desperation when a creditor knocks on your door. The last three times you pretended to be out, but this time, not only do you know that he knows you're in, but you also know that he knows that you know that he knows you're in. Anyway you've got to face him, and he's been looking forward to it for days...

If your wife glances more than once at a suspiciously biological or cosmetic stain on your clothing, you don't need the predictive powers of Nostradamus to see ten seconds into the future. You are going to be in some difficulty.

To wait, quaking, for the inevitable accusation in any of the above scenarios, and then to give a hesitant mumbled apology is to invite catastrophe of the sort you can imagine yourself without any help from us. What we can do is to recommend excuses, classified under the Diversion of Blame Technique and Smokescreen Technique which should cover each one of the wide variety of situations in which we layabouts find ourselves. For those whose habit it is to live life on the edge of credulity we have provided a Desperation classification of excuses.

These may be successful depending on the gullability of the audience but we cannot in all honesty recommend them. For the truly pathetic amongst us we have classified one last line of defence - The Last Resort Excuse - in which the obviously ludicrous comes to the fore, may gain you time for as long as your audience is a lively saint who is kind to dumb animals. With luck they might regard you as one. One last point, these excuses must not be simply recited - they must be "delivered", and the panache and precision with which you do so will determine your ultimate fate.

Remember that the truly successful excuser is never regarded as such, because the thought that he is being economical with the truth never occurs to others. They merely wonder why they can never pin him down.

Dare you take the risk of not having a ready excuse?

Can you think of an excuse for not buying this book?

You're panting, and as you run up the stairs you hope the boss won't spot the fact that you should have been there 15 minutes ago. You decide to postpone that visit to the john until later, but as you enter, you're stabbed by two eyes which flick to the clock on the wall and then back to you. Your absence has been noticed, and the owner of the eyes is walking towards you.

WHAT'S YOUR EXCUSE?

Diversion of Blame Technique

1. My pet goat ate the leg of my suit trousers.

2. I discovered the baker lying dead on the floor of his shop.

3. I couldn't get rid of three early morning mormons.

Smokescreen Technique

1. I got pestered by this woman who is convinced I am her dead son.

2. The Water pump in my aquarium burst and I had to rescue my tropical fish.

3. I took my first epileptic fit, had to buy onion.

Desperation Technique

1. The Taxi driver had a heart attack.

2. My Mother-in-law set fire to her bed.

3. I caught the postman stealing cucumbers from my greenhouse.

Last Resort

* I couldn't get out of my house as my neighbour was holding seige.

You know you had to be there on the dot or else you'd miss the start of a film. But you've done it, haven't you? Your hair is still a bit wet from the shower, and you hope the chemicals you applied to your armpits are doing their job. Calm down the breathing. There she is. She doesn't look impressed by your arrival.

DIVERSION OF BLAME TECHNIQUE

1. I swerved to avoid this dog and ran over a cyclist.

2. I lost my credit cards.

3. The wheels got stolen off my car.

SMOKESCREEN TECHNIQUE

1. I was taking part in Radio Phone-In.

2. The upstairs roof fell in.

3. I got pushed through shop window.

DESPERATION TECHNIQUE

1. There was a rabid dog in the garden. I couldn't get out.

2. A flock of starlings have taken up residence in the loft.

3. Someone had left an old double wardrobe against my front door and I couldn't get out.

LAST RESORT

*   I found a dead body in my garden.

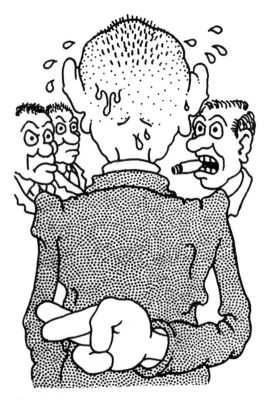

Everybody else is there; in fact everybody else has been there for quite some time, doing very little else apart from waiting for you, and indulging in some strained conversation. It's not so much that which bothers you, but more the fact that this conversation stops as you come in the room, and all the eyes turn to you, with question marks in them.
Your move.

DIVERSION OF BLAME TECHNIQUE

1. I got bitten by a tramp, and I had to get anti-tetanus injection.

2. My car got sandwiched in, and I couldn't get out.

3. A woman handed me a baby in the station, and disappeared.

SMOKESCREEN TECHNIQUE

1. I took an old Polish man who couldn't speak English to the police station. He thought he was in Switzerland, he must have gotten on the wrong plane

2. My shoe fell off in the rush for train, And I had to go home.

3. I was witness to a serious accident.

DESPERATION TECHNIQUE

1. An angry neighbour had deflated my tyres.

2. I have discovered an old painting in the loft, and I had to organise insurance.

3. I was interviewed by a Japanese TV crew.

LAST RESORT

* I got arrested for suspected shoplifting.

Being Late for a Wedding

You know that people make jokes about this, but you're quite aware of the fact that the bride's sense of humour is not likely to be receptive to anything she might have found funny yesterday. The sweat is prickling your back, and you wish that the red light conspiracy at the traffic lights, would stop, and you wish taxis had turbochargers, and you wish that you were even five minutes earlier. What on earth will you say when you arrive.

WHAT'S YOUR EXCUSE?

DIVERSION OF BLAME TECHNIQUE

1. I got cornered by the Moonies.

2. The bath fell through the floor.

3. I found a mouse in the breakfast cereal, and I had to take it to the vet.

SMOKESCREEN TECHNIQUE

1. I got involved in hold-up at the bank.

2. I found a badger in the car.

3. I chased a hit and run driver.

DESPERATION TECHNIQUE

1. I found a baby in the garden.

2. Next door's caravan exploded.

3. The Police stopped me for going through red light.

LAST RESORT

* I got chased by pack of wild dogs.

Not paying Taxes

We all know that the wheels of state must be oiled,
but you fail to see why it should be withsomething
you regard as being of only marginally less importance
that your blood - your money. You haven't just
been ducking and diving - you're evasive maneuvers
would not have disgraced Lord Lucan. Now you've
been caught by the person you dread more than a
wasp in your snorkel - the taxman, who would like
to ask a question or two.

WHAT'S YOUR EXCUSE?

Diversion of Blame Technique

1. I'm not paying because it is unfair.

2. I don't use local amenities, so I'm not paying.

3. I'm needing money to get the car converted for my brother's wheelchair.

Smokescreen Technique

1. I thought this tax was being scrapped.

2. I'm sure I've paid already.

3. I'm a vegeterian, I'm not paying.

Desperation Technique

1. I need the money to get the wife's haemorrhoids done.

2. I kept all the accounts on home computer which got burgled.

3. I've been in hospital having heart surgery.

Last Resort

• I am not from this planet.

Your credit problems and credibility problems are closely linked here - you need more materials, but you haven't paid for the last lot yet. What you have to do is explain why you haven't settled the account, and make it sound good enough for more credit to be extended. That way you can make the next payment on your Porsche.

WHAT'S YOUR EXCUSE?

DIVERSION OF BLAME TECHNIQUE

1. The computer is not working.

2. We're being investigated by the IRS and they've frozen the account.

3. My Wife has raided the bank account and run off with the bank manager.

SMOKESCREEN TECHNIQUE

1. I posted the cheque this morning.

2. My partner is not here to sign the cheque.

3. Someone has payed me with a cheque which bounced. So our account is in the red.

DESPERATION TECHNIQUE

1. My secretary is having a severe attack of amnesia. She doesn't even recognise me.

2. I'm waiting for the exchange rate to improve.

3. There was a fire in the office. All accounts were destroyed.

LAST RESORT

* The computer programme has been erased by mistake.

The letter from the Building Society is lurking in your pocket as you wait in the manager's office. He'll be there in a few minutes to discuss the fact that you haven't paid your dues for three months. You've heard that such things can be rescheduled at the managers discretion, so you need a strategy, but that holiday to the Seychelles last month maybe wan't such a good idea.

Diversion of Blame Technique

1. There's been a death in the family and I've had to pay the funeral expenses.

2. I lost my cheque card and someone has spent up to my full credit limit.

3. I need the money to get the doors widened for my daughter's new wheelchair.

Smokescreen Technique

1. Interpol have frozen my bank account.

2. My mother-in-law needs a new false leg.

3. I've been held by the police for the last three weeks on suspicion of belonging to a terrorist organisation.

Desperation Technique

1. There was a fire and my wallet got destroyed with my money in it.

2. I need the money to bail my son out of a Turkish jail.

3. My wife sent all our money to a very worthwhile charity.

Last Resort

* I'm in the middle of a nervous breakdown, please leave me alone or I'll kill myself..

Bouncing Cheques

It's the personal touch that's embarassing. If someone had written you letters about it you could have at least lost them, but now he's in front of you, holding the cheque you wrote a fortnight ago - cruelly stamped by the bank. Your personal integrity is at stake here. It's not to say that you've got any, but the point is that you want other people to think you have. And he looks hurt and annoyed. And he's bigger than you.

WHAT'S YOUR EXCUSE?

DIVERSION OF BLAME TECHNIQUE

1. We just discovered that my secretary has been stealing money out of the account to sustain her heroin habit.

2. The bank's computer was responsible.

3. There's a new manager at the bank who dosen't know about my arrangement.

SMOKESCREEN TECHNIQUE

1. I don't understand it. There's thousands in that account.

2. The cheque was drawn on the wrong account.

3. The bank manager is just getting me back since I beat him at bridge last week.

DESPERATION TECHNIQUE

1. Our computer has been making mistakes.

2. We have moved our bank account to a more understanding bank.

3. We have just discovered the accountant we started three months ago is not an account ant at all. He's an ex-female impersonator who went by the name Fifi a' la' mor.

LAST RESORT

* Someone has hacked into our computer and stolen all our money .

Not Paying Pocket Money

His little hands are outstretched and the eyes are getting bigger by the second. The problem is one of understanding the realities of life, such as your need to pour moderate amounts of alcohol down the inside of your neck, or your need to make periodic investments at the turf accountants. You don't really mind giving them their pocket money, but not right now. Maybe after the 2.30 at Kempton tomorrow.

WHAT'S YOUR EXCUSE?

Diversion of Blame Technique

1. I didn't get paid this week.

2. I lost my wallet.

3. I got robbed.

Smokescreen Technique

1. Last week I paid you two weeks, had you forgotten?

2. I left your pocket money on the table, you're sister must have stolen it.

3. I'm saving up to buy you a very big present.

Desperation Technique

1. I need the money for an operation for your mother.

2. I've sent the money away to the save the children fund.

3. I used the money to buy you a puppy, but it died on the way home.

Last Resort

* Mummy has stolen all my money, I think she's taking drugs again.

Not Paying Restaurant Bills

The second cup of coffee is getting cold - not that you wanted it anyway, but it delayed the inevitable. You must choose whether to spend the rest of your life here ordering coffee or whether to deal with the consequences of not having succeeded in finding your wallet, despite examining all of your pockets at least seven hopeful times. That waiter is approaching again, and there are plenty of witnesses.

WHAT'S YOUR EXCUSE?

DIVERSION OF BLAME TECHNIQUE

1. Michael Caine said I could eat here for free.

2. One of the other guests has picked my pocket.

3. The guy at the door said we had won a free meal.

SMOKESCREEN TECHNIQUE

1. I just can't bring myself to pay for the pig fodder I've just eaten.

2. There was a slug in my lasagne.

3. There was egg yolk between the prongs of my fork.

DESPERATION TECHNIQUE

1. What do you mean? I bloody paid you ten minutes ago.

2. I got mugged in the toilet.

3. I'm from Egon Ronay.

LAST RESORT

* Shout loudly - A rat just ran over my foot.!

Unfaithfulness

Your partners face has been crossed by the merest twitch of a frown at the sight of a suspiciously biological or cosmetic stain on your clothing. Up to this point your philandering tendencies have, you believe, been unnoticed, but this is a situation which calls for some quick thinking. Or some quick lying.

WHAT'S YOUR EXCUSE?

DIVERSION OF BLAME TECHNIQUE

1. It was a chemical thing, it just happened.

2. I was drunk, I can't remember a thing.

3. She begged me for it.

SMOKESCREEN TECHNIQUE

1. She makes me feel special.

2. It was dark, I was sure it was you.

3. She talks dirty and you don't.

DESPERATION TECHNIQUE

1. I only did it for a laugh.

2. I did it to stop her pestering me.

3. I only did it to prove that I was still macho.

LAST RESORT

* I was married to her in an earlier life.

*When you are asked "How was it for you darling?"
It is not generally considered good form to answer
"Bloody awful actually." Good manners may
dictate white lies. However, if you have just
experienced what might be termed an anti-climax,
and your partner is aware that this is the case, then
an excuse is the answer. That is, if you want the
chance to try again sometime......*

WHAT'S YOUR EXCUSE?

Diversion of Blame Technique

1. I can normally perform no problem after eight beers. It must be the peanuts I ate

2. I think I might have a dislocated scrotum.

3. Dr Ruth said fifteen seconds is the average time for a lay. So you've really had an extra eight seconds.

Smokescreen Technique

1. There must be something wrong with you.

2. I've got a lot of worries at the moment.

3. The doctor said I shouldn't exert myself too much.

Desperation Technique

1. I can't understand it, my penis is normally twice this size.

2. Although I like you a lot, I don't think my penis likes you.

3. I'm going to speak to the trading standards people about those Spanish Flies, they look and taste to me like normal bluebottles.

Last Resort

* Did you know I can lick my eyebrows.

Caught wearing partners Undies

We couldn't begin to suggest why you have been doing this - well, we might, but we're not going to. The point is that your secret has been revealed, and unless you have an excellent genuine reason which will allow you to escape some severe mockery, either prepare to blush or accept some suggestions.

WHAT'S YOUR EXCUSE?

DIVERSION OF BLAME TECHNIQUE

1. They say it's the only way to stop smoking.

2. It reminds me of when I was in boarding school.

3. I'm practising for halloween.

SMOKESCREEN TECHNIQUE

1. I've just bought these for you and wanted to see what they looked like on.

2. I want to be a model.

3. I'm auditioning for a play.

DESPERATION TECHNIQUE

1. They say this will help to increase my understanding of the female species.

2. I wanted to know what it felt like.

3. I think we should have a talk. There are few things you should know.

LAST RESORT

* Would you start calling me Tracy. ?

Caught Flashing

*Was it deliberate? Of course not - at least not in the
way that they are saying so. You don't have time
for indiscriminate exhibitionism.   However, you
are about to be nicked unless you can come up with
a realativly harmless explanation. The policeman
is approaching you, and it's time to take the initiative.*

WHAT'S YOUR EXCUSE?

DIVERSION OF BLAME TECHNIQUE

1. I'm doing it for a bet.

2. I forgot to put on my trousers.

3. There was a wasp under my coat.

SMOKESCREEN TECHNIQUE

1. I am a walking piece of art.

2. I needed to air my parts.

3. Underpants and trousers are too restrictive.

DESPERATION TECHNIQUE

1. I can't wear underpants because of my piles.

2. Since I've put this "Penis Enlarging Gel" on it feels as if I'm on fire.

3. I like to make women laugh.

LAST RESORT

*   God told me to do it.

Soft or hard-core, it doesn't matter.   What is important is the potential reaction of whoever it is who has discovered your possession of the naughty magazines.   Even a comparitively innocuous publication which would not raise an eyebrow in hearty male company might well raise hell if dropped in view of a feminist campaigner.   So let's say you've done it - maybe you were taking your sandwiches out of your briefcase, or else it's dropped from behind your copy of Homes and Gardens. "What on Earth are you doing with that?" is the cry.

DIVERSION OF BLAME TECHNIQUE

1. I'm an aspiring amatuer photographer. and wanted some tips.

2. I'm a painter and I can't afford to pay for models.

3. Someone put them through my letterbox.

SMOKESCREEN TECHNIQUE

1. I wanted to see what all the fuss was about.

2. I'm knitting a quilt and wanted some ideas.

3. My ex-wife is in this film.

DESPERATION TECHNIQUE

1. I just confiscated these from some young kids.

2. I'm having a terrible job satisfying my girlfriend, and wanted some new ideas.

3. I'm keeping them for a friend.

LAST RESORT

* I'm thinking of joining the St. John's Ambulance Brigade and wanted to brush up on my anatomy.

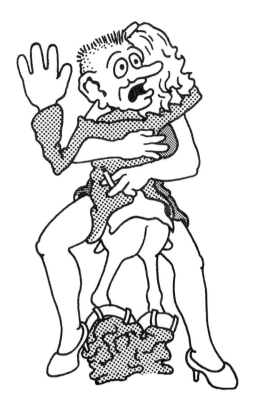

In former times, society was much more hypocritical about such things, and many a blind eye was turned, rightly or wrongly, to gentlemen who indulged in this kind of illicit activity. Nowadays, any man caught in this situation is regarded as at best an object of some derision. We mean no harm to the ladies involved in prostitution, but if you are a man and if you are caught, you'd better have a story ready. The Sunday papers could enjoy it otherwise.

WHAT'S YOUR EXCUSE?

DIVERSION OF BLAME TECHNIQUE

1. My wife won't do half the things that Candy will.

2. She said she needed the money to buy her husband a new-battery powered wheelchair.

3. She said she loved me and wanted my baby.

SMOKESCREEN TECHNIQUE

1. My wife won't do it with me because of my bad breath.

2. I was cold and needed heating up.

3. I was only doing the girl a favour. She said that business was slack.

DESPERATION TECHNIQUE

1. She's an old girlfriend and I was giving her one for old time's sake.

2. I'm a vicar in the early stages of reforming this poor girl back to the way of the Lord.

3. I'm writing a book and needed to know what having sex was like.

LAST RESORT

* She said if I was any good I would get my money back.

"Darling, my headache has gone now", she says, seductively stroking your elbow. Cause for celebration? No, not really, because you're not in the mood. Can you say that out loud? No, of course you can't. Since although women rejecting men has long since become cliched, men had better have a pretty good reason, as a woman is not likely to enjoy rejection. She will be hurt - or livid. So for either the best or the worst of reasons, your excuse had better be good.

WHAT'S YOUR EXCUSE?

DIVERSION OF BLAME TECHNIQUE

1. I don't want any more children. Eleven is enough.

2. I've got a rash after sitting on a public toilet seat.

3. I've got a terrible migraine.

SMOKESCREEN TECHNIQUE

1. I don't have any condoms.

2. Sex with you is just so intense and pleasurable I'm going to punish myself and not do it tonight.

3. I got overdosed with radiation this afternoon and have been told not to have sex until tomorrow.

DESPERATION TECHNIQUE

1. I think I might have VD.

2. I've got a terrible pain in my bottom.

3. My left testicle is throbbing, I think I might have cancer.

LAST RESORT

* I've got no feeling in my penis, I hope I'm not getting polio.

A perversion is something sexual your partner hasn't really thought of doing before, and therefore can encompass activities ranging from "keeping the light on" to things which we ourselves have never thought of doing. However, at some point you're going to have to bring up the subject of your own particular kink. You'll put it carefully, but if she reacts with reluctance or horror, have an explanation ready.

WHAT'S YOUR EXCUSE?

DIVERSION OF BLAME TECHNIQUE

1. I was beaten as a child.

2. At least a sheep can't nag at you.

3. We all used to do this at public school.

SMOKESCREEN TECHNIQUE

1. There's nothing better for the circulation than a good sound spanking.

2. They say getting chained up helps prevent arthritis.

3. Getting whipped reminds me of when I was a lion-tamer.

DESPERATION TECHNIQUE

1. I only have this blow up rubber doll for a bit of company.

2. Everybody keeps things in their bottom.

3. I've always wanted to be a horse.

LAST RESORT

* I'm a high court judge.

Voyeurism

Think of the last flush of panic as she turns her head and looks into your eyes. She knows that your telescope has been pointing at her, or that you've been looking in her window. You can't run away, or else your description will be in the evening paper - she might even recognise you! Your story had better be convincing.

WHAT'S YOUR EXCUSE?

DIVERSION OF BLAME TECHNIQUE

1. I wanted to see what your decor was like.

2. I am looking for my gerbil.

3. I heard someone screaming.

SMOKESCREEN TECHNIQUE

1. I was watching your TV because mine was bust.

2. I was thinking of getting the same double glazing as you.

3. I was watching an owl.

DESPERATION TECHNIQUE

1. I thought I recognised you from television.

2. I'm chasing a squirrel. Which has been stealing underwear from our washing line.

3. I'm lost.

LAST RESORT

* God told me to watch over you.

Buying Womens Clothing

A large number of men have done it, but even if it is a dressing gown for your granny, isn't there a certain twinge of uneasiness there? The assistant comes up to you from behind the racks of naughty looking underclothes and asks if she can help. You notice a trace of a different question in her voice. Are you kinky or what? Maybe it's paranoia, but you need to say something, don't you?

WHAT'S YOUR EXCUSE?

Diversion of Blame Technique

1. It's a present for the wife.

2. They're a present for my cousin - he's one of them you know.

3. I'm making a life size puppet for the local orphanage.

Smokescreen Technique

1. I'm sending them to Ethiopia.

2. I'm a fireman and I want to test how flame retardant they are.

3. They're for my sister.

Desperation Technique

1. I just love a bargain.

2. I'm a window dresser and these are for a mannequin.

3. It's my company that manufactures these, and I need to take them back because they're flawed.

Last Resort

* I'm in a play.

Speeding

You know you should have been looking. Come to that, you know you shouldn't have been speeding in the first place. But now you're stopped, and the police officer with the flourescent jacket is walking towards your car. He motions you to wind down your window, and he's not smiling.

WHAT'S YOUR EXCUSE?

DIVERSION OF BLAME TECHNIQUE

1. There was a wasp in the car and it was attacking me.

2. The accelerator stuck.

3. I've got a cramp in my leg.

SMOKESCREEN TECHNIQUE

1. I've just had a minor epileptic fit.

2. I've lost my contact lenses and I can't see the speedo.

3. I was trying to catch up with the guy in front. I recognise him from LA Law.

DESPERATION TECHNIQUE

1. I have to get home for my insulin.

2. I'm desperate to go to the toilet - I think I've got Beri - Beri.

3. My truss has slipped, and while trying to readjust it I lost my concentration.

LAST RESORT

*   Is that your money lying there.

Drunk Driving

In our opinion, anyone caught at this deserves all they get, but true to our mission of providing ammunition for the errant citizen, here are some offerings, and much good may they do you!

DIVERSION OF BLAME TECHNIQUE

1. I've been drinking grapefruit juice all night. Someone must have slipped a few Vodka's in them.

2. I haven't been drinking. I must be allergic to the chemicals the dry cleaner has used on my masonic apron.

3. I've just buried my dear old Mother.

SMOKESCREEN TECHNIQUE

1. My metabolism turns sugar into alcohol.

2. I was so thirsty the only thing I had to drink was this bottle of whisky.

3. I can't give you a blood sample. I'm a Jehovah's Witness.

DESPERATION TECHNIQUE

1. I've just won a million in the lottery and I'm on my way to the job - centre to see if I can find an ex-policeman to work for me for a thousand a week.

2. I've just left a meeting with the Chief of Police.

3. I'm a whisky taster.

LAST RESORT

* I'm a priest, some bastard must have spiked the alter wine.

Thieving

You're guilty. You know you're guilty. You thought you would get away with it and you've been caught red-handed. I mean, you didn't steal very much. If it goes to court the sentence will not be over long. But your name will be in the paper, and you do not need this kind of advertising! Maybe you can talk your way out of it.

WHAT'S YOUR EXCUSE?

DIVERSION OF BLAME TECHNIQUE

1. It's for my neighbour who's a cripple.

2. I haven't eaten for three days.

3. It was just sitting there and nobody seemed to appreciate it.

SMOKESCREEN TECHNIQUE

1. I'm only borrowing it.

2. A woman asked me to fetch it for her. She can't get in with her wheelchair.

3. I was only taking it outside to see it in daylight.

DESPERATION TECHNIQUE

1. I had this when I came in.

2. I need this 56lb of lead to make fishing weights for the orphanage.

3. I was just taking them away to photograph them.

LAST RESORT

* God told me to take it.

Whoops! There it goes, or rather, there it's gone. It's not your intention to wreck the precious and fragile possessions of others, but the people who know you best velcro their ornaments to the mantelpiece, and give you tea in a plastic mug. Now you've done it again, and as your eyes go from the wreckage on the road to the eyes of the other driver is that a tear and a quivering lower lip you see?

WHAT'S YOUR EXCUSE?

DIVERSION OF BLAME TECHNIQUE

1. I ran into the back of his car because he gave me the V sign.

2. I couldn't see him for the Sun/Moon.

3. He was going so fast I didn't see him.

SMOKESCREEN TECHNIQUE

1. I stopped to adjust my seat.

2. I heard a coughing noise in the back.

3. I was just testing my brakes.

DESPERATION TECHNIQUE

1. I always go round the roundabout this way.

2. He was just indicating to turn and that's why I pulled out.

3. I didn't brake that hard.

LAST RESORT

* I've just had a very religous experience, God was just telling me a few things about how he wants me to improve the lot of the blue whale.

*It's a Free Country isn't it? You have every right
to protest and inform others of your feelings!
The local police disagree, having been summoned
by a group of partying football playerscomplaining
about the noise you're making which was disturbing
their singing. As the boys in blue appear the red
haze disappears from your eyes.*

WHAT'S YOUR EXCUSE?

Diversion of Blame Technique

1. It's these pills I've been taking.

2. I'm from a ghetto, I don't know any better.

3. I'm exercising my basic rights to demonstrate.

Smokescreen Technique

1. I'm doing a Nigerian fertility dance.

2. I'm not causing a disturbance, I'm Praising the Lord.

3. He said he was going to beat up a policeman so I stopped him.

Desperation Technique

1. He said Norman Schwarzkopf had a head like a King Edward potatoe.

2. He said I had bad breath.

3. He said my wife had a face like a horses's ass.

Last Resort

* I am very very angry at the Hubble Telescope not working properly.

It all started when you went to the pub for a quiet drink and met some rowdy friends, and eventually you regarded a drinking race with halfpints a reasonable thing to do. The fact that it was halfpints of Tequila only made it more challenging. But you've only a vague recollection of events as you stand before the court.

DIVERSION OF BLAME TECHNIQUE

1. My wife has just passed away.

2. My wife has just given birth to twins.

3. My son has just been voted Poet of the Year.

SMOKESCREEN TECHNIQUE

1. I've just been voted onto the committee as chief fundraiser for the Retired Judges Appeal.

2. I've just been promoted to the head of the Police complaints department.

3. I'm celebrating my divorce.

DESPERATION TECHNIQUE

1. I've just been told I'm terminally ill and I've only got four weeks to live.

2. I'm celebrating my sons promotion to Chief of Police.

3. I've just come back, from an audience with the Queen.

LAST RESORT

* I've just come back from the dead.

The polite smile of the officer at the Spot Check changes to a look of puzzlement when he sees a clot like you sitting behind the wheel of a hot sports coupe like this. Simultaneously you feel the threat of a noisy commotion in your underwear because you know that this car is even hotter than it looks and you will have to answer some very probing questions.

WHAT'S YOUR EXCUSE?

DIVERSION OF BLAME TECHNIQUE

1. I thought it was mine.

2. I took it to pursue a criminal.

3. I was just moving it out of the sun in case it melted.

SMOKESCREEN TECHNIQUE

1. I had to take it to get to hospital.

2. I took the car so I could take a wee tramp for a tour of the Scottish Highlands.

3. The owner said I could have a spin in it.

DESPERATION TECHNIQUE

1. I'm a member of the green movement and I was taking this car to get it converted to lead free.

2. I took the car so I could take three orphans on a driving tour.

3. I was just trying it out, I might buy one.

LAST RESORT

* An old woman collapsed on the sidewalk so I went and stole the car. When I went to get her to take her to hospital she was gone. So having gone to the bother of taking the car I thought I might just drive around and see if I could do a good deed for someone.

Burglary

No one who has ever had their house done over would wish it on anyone else. Nevertheless those who wish to follow the dishonourable trade of "gentleman burglar" may find the following useful if they are confronted by the occupants of the house, and do not, of course, wish to indulge in any unsavoury activity of a violent nature . This apart from being extra offensive would lead to legal action being taken against the aggressor.

WHAT'S YOUR EXCUSE?

Diversion of Blame Technique

1. I thought it was my own house.

2. I was looking for our lost dalmatian.

3. I was just getting some ideas on the decoration.

Smokescreen Technique

1. I was just trying to get warm. I'm freezing.

2. I was just wanting a drink of water.

3. Someone said there was a party on in here.

Desperation Technique

1. I heard someone shouting for help.

2. I thought he was having an affair with my wife.

3. I lived here in an earlier life and just wanted a look for old time's sake.

Last Resort

* I am an excorcist and I got funny vibes when I walked past here.

You've been hovering like an alcoholic, hyena/ vulture, waiting for dead glasses . The contents of which you intend disposing in a bid to further your ambition to become intoxicated in a method which is financially efficient. As you reach out for a promising looking whisky, a hairy hand grabs your wrist - very hard. The games up.

WHAT'S YOUR EXCUSE?

Diversion of Blame Technique

1. There was a fly doing the toilet in it.

2. There was lipstick on the glass.

3. I wanted to see if it tasted alright. It looked a bit cloudy to me.

Smokescreen Technique

1. It's my drink.

2. I thought you were finished.

3. You've had too many already.

Desperation Technique

1. I need it more than you.

2. I only wanted a sip.

3. I'm a necrophiliac.

Last Resort

* God told me to take it.

Taking someone's Coat

That's one benefit of being asked to leave a party early, you think to yourself, as you select from the pile of outer clothing on the bed an interesting tailored leather jacket. There's nobody else around. As you pass along the hallway on the way to the door, the owner of the jacket approaches you.

WHAT'S YOUR EXCUSE?

DIVERSION OF BLAME TECHNIQUE

1. Someone just handed me this.

2. I thought it was mine. I've got one just like this.

3. The host said I could just take it, sorry

SMOKESCREEN TECHNIQUE

1. I've left you mine, which is more your style.

2. There is a spider in this jacket. I'm taking it outside to shake it out .

3. It was lying in a heap, look at the creases in this

DESPERATION TECHNIQUE

1. I thought I overheard you saying you didn't like it.

2. I'm cold on account of my collapsed left lung.

3. I can't see. I've gone blind. Would you show me the front door please.

LAST RESORT

* I've brought your jacket. Would you like to see me home?

You've been congratulating yourself on your narrow escape and are enjoying a few drinks. Everybody will have left the church by now, you say to yourself, and I'm glad I'm not there - it would be so embarrassing. But it's not embarrassment you feel as your erstwhile fiancee's three brothers approach you, seemingly with a view to discussing the tearful plight of your jilted bride.

WHAT'S YOUR EXCUSE?

DIVERSION OF BLAME TECHNIQUE

1. The wheels got stolen off my car.

2. The barman has just had a nasty shock, so I'm consoling him.

3. Electricity pylon collapsed on a bus full of orphans on the way to the church so I stopped to help.

SMOKESCREEN TECHNIQUE

1. I suppose you're here to apologise on behalf of your sister.

2. I've got an incurable disease.

3. I thought it was tomorrow.

DESPERATION TECHNIQUE

1. There's an awful smell coming from my bottom, so I've decided not to go ahead with the wedding.

2. I've just found Jesus.

3. I'm going to Australia. Who are you? Who am I?

LAST RESORT

* I've just discovered I'm gay.

Not turning up to a Date

When you go into work on Monday morning you know that you'll have to face her, and be fairly nice to her, as she could make your life a misery there. "Nice" is not what you were to her on Saturday. She was waiting for you, and you had intended to meet her, but how were you to know that you would meet a far better prospect on the way there? You can hardly tell her that, especially as her vicious temper is matched only by the speed of her reactions. As you approach her desk, she is filing her nails - to a point.

WHAT'S YOUR EXCUSE?

Diversion of Blame Technique

1. Someone nailed my front door shut.

2. I was sick all night and semi - conscious, so I couldn't call.

3. A neighbour took a shot at me.

Smokescreen Technique

1. I got arrested on suspicion of murder.

2. Undercover cops raided my neighbour's house, and I had to help with some awkward questions.

3. Saturday? I thought it was next Saturday.

Desperation Technique

1. I lost my false teeth and was too embarassed to come.

2. My key broke in the lock. And I couln't get out.

3. I got my hand caught in the cigarette vending machine.

Last Resort

* I'm just not good enough for you.

It was fine when you were told by your boss to represent him at the meeting, even though he did say that everyone else was tied up and that you were the last resort. It was even better when you heard where the meeting was, because with that came the knowledge that you could hardly be expected in the office that day. It's not so good now though, as you will have to explain your non attendance. They will be unable to appreciate the attractions of golf on a sunny day over business.

WHAT'S YOUR EXCUSE?

Diversion of Blame Technique.

1. Someone slashed my tyres.

2. My mother in law got stuck in the bath.

3. My eyelids got stuck together.

Smokescreen Technique

1. Some idiots pet monkey escaped from their car and was running amok on the motorway.

2. Got an electric shock and have just come to.

3. The roads weren't the same as the map so I got lost.

Desperation Technique

1. Had to take mother in law to the detox unit.

2. Got followed by a van load of hell's angels.

3. My car was commandeered by a policeman following a hit and run driver.

Last Resort

* My brother died last night.

Not turning up in Court

You don't really have contempt for the court - it's really a very attractive building - but you are in serious trouble here, as magistrates and judges are known to take a dim view of your putting your own convenience before that of the law. The police arrived with a warrant for your arrest, but the look on their faces suggested a wistful regret that it was not for your death. Now you have to explain yourself.

WHAT'S YOUR EXCUSE?

DIVERSION OF BLAME TECHNIQUE

1. I helped an old woman who was being attacked by a doberman.

2. I got burgled last night.

3. I had toothache which made me dizzy.

SMOKESCREEN TECHNIQUE

1. I was being interviewed by Oprah Winfrey.

2. My son locked himself in the toilet

3. My car wouldn't start.

DESPERATION TECHNIQUE

1. I stopped an attempted robbery.

2. My wife's pet anaconda escaped and ate our neighbour's pit bull terrier.

3. The wife's hair has fallen out and she was hysterical.

LAST RESORT

* I had an appointment with the chiropidist.

Meeting With a Bank Manager

The "invitation" was polite but curt, asking you to attend at the manager's office to discuss your finances. As far as you're concerned, it might as well have been an invitation to discuss your luxury yachts or your private jets - you don't have any of these either. As you had a couple of extra commitments this month (fines etc) you decided to skip the ordeal, but a chance meeting with the manager in the street put paid to that. He enquires after your health. Or was it wealth?

WHAT'S YOUR EXCUSE?

DIVERSION OF BLAME TECHNIQUE

1. I caught the milkman burglarising the neighbours house.

2. Workmen have dug up the road in front of the driveway and I couldn't get the car out.

3. I found a rat in the milk carton and I had to alert the authorities.

SMOKESCREEN TECHNIQUE

1. My home brew exploded and ruined my new suit.

2. My garden shed got blown away, and I had to look for it.

3. I slipped on dog doo and had to change my clothes.

DESPERATION TECHNIQUE

1. I think capitalism is an outmoded and antiquated concept better suited to beings of lower intelligence than you and I.

2. I was helping an old woman across the road and she just died; just like that.

3. I knew you were a busy man, so I didn't like to bother you.

LAST RESORT

* Money - who needs it?

There are a number of reasons - even legitimate ones - for not coming to the phone. You might be busy working or it might be Accounts again about your expenses. You don't want to talk to him - but you don't want to fall out with him either.

DIVERSION OF BLAME TECHNIQUE

1. He's in a meeting.

2. He's on the toilet.

3. He's passed out. The ambulance man's trying to revive him with electric shocks.

SMOKESCREEN TECHNIQUE

1. He's on the other line. And there's two calls waiting.

2. He's got laryngitis and can't talk.

3. He's gone deaf in both ears, you'll have to write.

DESPERATION TECHNIQUE

1. He's superglued his hand to the chair.

2. He's not in at the moment.

3. He's outside shooting at the pigeons again.

LAST RESORT

* He's on the other line to his wife. I think she's run off again, cos he's sobbing.

If only your mother could see you now - come to that, you're glad neither she nor any of your friends can - it's so undignified. Friends are a bit thin on the ground though, as most of them have found you out for the lying dog you are. However, where there's life there's hope, and where there are people there's money. You need some drinking vouchers as your alcohol level has dropped dangerously and uncomfortably low. As you hold your hand to an affluent gent, what can you say to him when he asks you why?

WHAT'S YOUR EXCUSE?

DIVERSION OF BLAME TECHNIQUE

1. I'm just back from the war.

2. I gave all my money to charity.

3. I'm a reformed drug addict.

SMOKESCREEN TECHNIQUE

1. I don't want to steal.

2. It's not for myself you understand.

3. The money's to pay my Income Tax.

DESPERATION TECHNIQUE

1. I need the money for medicine.

2. I haven't eaten for six weeks.

3. I've only got days to live.

LAST RESORT

* Please.

Having a Messy House

You weren't expecting any visitors, but you've got them. Of course, it's at this time that an obscure law of disasters dictates that your house looks as if it has been stirred with a stick. As the newcomers look around thinking of something polite to say there is an embarassed silence. The ball's in your court.

WHAT'S YOUR EXCUSE?

Diversion of Blame Technique

1. We like it like this.

2. I'm sorting out some stuff for Oxfam.

3. Excuse the mess, it's the children.

Smokescreen Technique

1. We've just been burgled.

2. You've just missed a great party.

3. So, when was the last time you were raided?

Desperation Technique

1. I'm a manic depressive.

2. I'm on strike until my wife increases my allowance.

3. I'm just tidying up.

Last Resort

* Do you mind taking your shoes off. I've just cleaned?

Having a very Messy Garden

The Horticultural Society meeting next door seems to be going with a swing, and you're feeling quite laid back about the whole thing as you relax with a beer in the sunshine amidst the undergrowth of your own pit. But you get a twinge of conscience as one of the members leans over the fence and looks at you with a mixture of pity and distaste. He looks as if he's going to say something. It's time you got in there first.

DIVERSION OF BLAME TECHNIQUE

1. The gardener has hurt his back.

2. The lawnmower's in for repair.

3. Have you got kids?

SMOKESCREEN TECHNIQUE

1. When I last tried to mow the grass there was a snake in it.

2. You never see the Queen doing her garden do you?

3. You should let your garden get like this every three years.

DESPERATION TECHNIQUE

1. There is a shortage of long grass for local frogs and toads.

2. It's to let the grass take hold.

3. I'm starting a maze.

LAST RESORT

* Do you like my garden? I can't see it. I'm blind.

Punching your Neighbour

The man next door has been getting on your nerves
for years and has caused you nothing but trouble.
Refusing to lend you money,drink, his lawnmower
and wife and even calling the police when you tried
to borrow his car.
You've always preferred subtle tactics like writing
rude slogans on his lawn with paraquat
but this is the first time you have gone so far as to
punch his face. Will others understand?

WHAT'S YOUR EXCUSE?

DIVERSION OF BLAME TECHNIQUE

1. He belongs to a minority group.

2. He tripped and fell on my fist.

3. His wife stepped out of the way at the wrong time.

SMOKESCREEN TECHNIQUE

1. He's a communist.

2. He's a capitalist.

3. He deserved it.

DESPERATION TECHNIQUE

1. He hasn't cut his grass.

2. I don't like his wife

3. I don't like his dog.

LAST RESORT

* It was a case of mistaken identity. I thought he was someone else.

Your guests have been listening with some admiration to your new hi-fi, and the stomping from the living room tells you the party is going well. Between tracks, you hear a desperate hammering on your door. You answer it, only to see the sight of your neighbour in a dressing gown. He says something, but you can't hear it over the music. You close the door and join him on the terrace.

WHAT'S YOUR EXCUSE?

DIVERSION OF BLAME TECHNIQUE

1. My mother-in-law is deaf,
   so I had to turn it up.

2. There are so many people in here they
   can't all here it.

3. This is the kind of music that's got to be
   played loudly.

SMOKESCREEN TECHNIQUE

1. The volume controls broken.

2. What was that you were saying......

3. My hearing aid is in for repair.

DESPERATION TECHNIQUE

1. I thought we would share the experience
   with you.

2. Didn't you get your invitation?

3. I'm trying to scare the cockroaches
   away.

LAST RESORT

* Do you mind not banging on the door so
  loudly, there are people in here trying to
  sleep.

Not Having Double Glazing

Whether meant as a helpful suggestion to you as the householder, or as a piece of social point scoring, the question as to why you lack double glazing is often delivered in a pitying tone, and is about as helpful as suggesting to a tramp with sore feet that he use a taxi for transport instead. A good riposte is recommended, and has the added bonus of being adaptable to when those salesmen call you.

DIVERSION OF BLAME TECHNIQUE

1. If there is a build up of pressure in the house it could explode.

2. Since my neighbour got double glazing his wife has started speaking in tongues.

3. I've heard that people with double glazing can get cancer.

SMOKESCREEN TECHNIQUE

1. Those old windows have been lucky for us and we don't want to change them.

2. You've got double the cleaning to do.

3. My neighbour got a butterfly caught between his double glazing and it spoilt their Christmas dinner having to watch it die.

DESPERATION TECHNIQUE

1. Double glazing keeps the smell in.

2. The same day my cousin got double glazing he lost his job.

3. We cannot pay our mortgage - how do you expect us to afford double glazing?

LAST RESORT

* We are saving up at the moment for a torch - call us back in three months.

Ruining Dinner

You followed the recipe closely - or at least you think you did - but as the result would be turned down by a starving pig it's not likely that your cooking is going to receive any compliments. It's all been caused by your basic incompetence in the kitchen, but do you really want to admit that?

WHAT'S YOUR EXCUSE?

Diversion of Blame Technique

1. The oven door stuck and I couldn't get it open.

2. There must be a misprint in the recipe book.

3. It's meant to taste ethnic and burnt.

Smokescreen Technique

1. It wasn't like that halk an hour ago. If you'd arrived on time it would have been perfect.

2. The microwave has over reacted.

3. My wife was supposed to watch it.

Desperation Technique

1. Burnt garlic is good for your hair.

2. Since those Mormons were here this morning I've felt really funny, sort of like in a trance. I wonder if they've cast a spell on me.

3. These new pots are just the pits.

Last Resort

* I'm on this new cabon diet. Its so healthy.

When you've told all your stories, and they've told all of theirs, and your eyes are straying to the clock on the wall, it's probably unwise to follow the example of a gentleman of our acquaintance who announced to his dinner guests, "I'm off to bed. It's time all you bastards went home." Avoid social ostracism - drop a gentle hint.

WHAT'S YOUR EXCUSE?

DIVERSION OF BLAME TECHNIQUE

1. You'll have to go it's time for my enema.

2. There's our new neighbour coming up the garden, he's a nice man for a double murderer.

3. Your mother will be in shortly. I hope she doesn't bring that horrible little man with the head lice with her again.

SMOKESCREEN TECHNIQUE

1. Careful theres a rat that comes out here about now.

2. Oh, Oh I feel a particularly violent epileptic fit coming on.

3. You'll have to excuse me but it's time for my mother-in-law's bed bath.

DESPERATION TECHNIQUE

1. Oh shit, the anaconda's loose.

2. The cockroaches will be out any minute now.

3. Does anyone fancy a farting competition.

LAST RESORT

* Does anyone fancy a seance, to see if we can call up the devil.

When it's 11.30am and you answer the doorbell in your night attire which has in all probability fallen open in unfortunate places, a look of surprise and righteous accusation may come over the face of the caller. You're hardly displaying a positive attitude to life, the world, and the work ethic, are you?

WHAT'S YOUR EXCUSE?

DIVERSION OF BLAME TECHNIQUE

1. My alarm clock's broken.

2. I've just got in from a business trip and I'm still on Japanese time.

3. What are you doing calling here in the middle of the night? Why is the sun shining?

SMOKESCREEN TECHNIQUE

1. Your wife kept me up all night.

2. Would you care to join me?

3. I'm under hypnosis.

DESPERATION TECHNIQUE

1. I'm on hunger strike and therefore very weak.

2. If I stand up my piles will fall out.

3. I'm thinking about Jesus.

LAST RESORT

* I've got terrible pains in my right nipple.

At the start you thought you'd just tap a pint from a tolerant acquaintance. That went fine. It went even better when his friend came in and bought you another. It was heaven when his friends from the football club came in. At least it was, for an hour or three. You've been spinning out the last inch of your pint for 15 minutes now, but the well dried up. There are 11 empty glasses on the table. You have no money, 22 eyes are concentrated on you, and the conversation is dying.

WHAT'S YOUR EXCUSE?

DIVERSION OF BLAME TECHNIQUE

1. Damnation, There's a hole in my pocket.

2. I wish my brother would hurry up with my money.

3. Shit, my gold VISA card expired yesterday.

SMOKESCREEN TECHNIQUE

1. I bought the fourth round.

2. I'll need to get back to the Hospice.

3. Could you excuse me while I get money out of the car.

DESPERATION TECHNIQUE

1. OK who's taken my wallet?

2. Start crying.

3. Leave via the toilet window.

LAST RESORT

* Does anyone want a go at my bottom.?

You can try telling yourself that you didn't really want the job anyway, bu you know it's a lie. It's like a typing mistake - only this typing mistake has wiped out everybody's wages for next week and the firm's orders for the next year. You actually erased the disk about an hour ago and have been playing Space Invaders ever since. Now the boss is calling for the file.

WHAT'S YOUR EXCUSE?

Diversion of Blame Technique

1. It wasn't me.

2. The computer told me to do it.

3. There was a blinding flash and the next thing was the screen went blank.

Smokescreen Technique

1. I thought I was saving it.

2. I got the D: drive mixed up with the C: drive.

3. I spilt my coffee on it and I'm really sorry.

Desperation Technique

1. The computer erased it by itself.

2. The computer has a suicide wish.

3. There was this really funny noise then nothing.

Last Resort

* God told me to do it.

Since you very often make errors of a major nature people tend not to give you complicated things to do. On this occasion the foreman of the engineering department told you to drill a 10mm hole, 25mm deep in a piece of metal. This component is vital, but he reckoned that even you could do such a simple job.. He was wrong. You drilled a 25mm hole, 10mm deep. You could offer to pay for it, but since you went for a smoke, you have ruined 3000 of them. Maybe its police protection you need, rather than an excuse. Try anyway.

WHAT'S YOUR EXCUSE?

DIVERSION OF BLAME TECHNIQUE

1. Someone has been tampering with this while I've been at the toilet.

2. It must have vibrated free when those trucks rumbled past.

3. Have you been buying that cheap wood again?

SMOKESCREEN TECHNIQUE

1. The control panel has melted inside.

2. There was a slight earth tremour last night and it must have damaged the controls.

3. It was straight when I started.

DESPERATION TECHNIQUE

1. They're near enough.

2. This machine is possessed.

3. I didn't do this.

LAST RESORT

* You told me to do it like this!

You don't have any holidays to take this year, even though it's only May, so that option won't work. The only thing left to try is the boss's good nature. If you have a good reason for wanting time off, maybe he'll forget for a second who he's talking to.

DIVERSION OF BLAME TECHNIQUE

1. I have to take my crippled neighbour to the bus for Lourdes.

2. I have to take over from my wife for the day while she is getting a new caliper fitted.

3. My mother in law is possessed again and I have to be there for the excorsist comeing.

SMOKESCREEN TECHNIQUE

1. I have to undergo tests I think I have an incurable disease.

2. Your wife says you're mean and will never give me time off but I said she had misjudged you.

3. I've been asked to meet some people in Whitehall regarding my Iranian neighbours.

DESPERATION TECHNIQUE

1. A film crew are coming round to the house, I could mention your name if you like.

2. An old gypsy cursed the house yesterday and I've got to find her to buy the friggin' clothes pegs.

3. My penis has trebled in size and I'm going to make the most of it before it reverts to normal.

LAST RESORT

* People from Mensa are coming round to meet me in person.

The first four times you did this on the computer, you had the excuse that you were only learning the job, but since then you've been on the training course, that didn't do a lot of good on its own, so the office smartarse (someone who actually knows how to use a damned computer) has been keeping an eye on you. You've now had more tuition time than a brain surgeon, and you were left alone for an hour. The fact is, the file's gone.

WHAT'S YOUR EXCUSE?

DIVERSION OF BLAME TECHNIQUE

1. It was there half an hour ago.

2. Someone has nicked it.

3. There was a blast of wind and it blew out of the window.

SMOKESCREEN TECHNIQUE

1. It got put in the internal mail.

2. It must have fallen in the bin, which got emptied an hour ago.

3. I put it in the shredder by mistake.

DESPERATION TECHNIQUE

1. The office junior had it last.

2. The window cleaner must've taken it.

3. When I came back from the toilet it was gone, I thought you had it.

LAST RESORT

* Looks like industrial espionage to me.

Absenteeism

*It's lunchtime, and having enjoyed a few pints with
your chums, you are all ambling towards your club
to while away the afternoon hours. Unfortunately
you all amble into a gentleman with a briefcase
obviously coming from a meeting involving the
industry in which you work. You know this
because he's your boss. Your chums have all
ambled off and as his gaze transfixes you, you feel
like a mouse in front of a cobra.*

WHAT'S YOUR EXCUSE?

DIVERSION OF BLAME TECHNIQUE

1. Today's Saturday isn't it?

2. We got burgled last night.

3. My brother has just been Knighted and we've been celebrating since yesterday.

SMOKESCREEN TECHNIQUE

1. Today is a public holiday.

2. I've just come out of coma.

3. Someone's stolen our greenhouse

DESPERATION TECHNIQUE

1. There was a strange family in our house when I came home from work yesterday, they say the house is theirs. We've spent all night sleeping in the garden shed.

2. The wife's discovered she's only got one week to live so I've been getting her insured.

3. My seven year old son left a note to say he is away to join the circus.

LAST RESORT

* Would you like to join us for a drink?

You might think they'd be grateful. After all, the material was in good order, the correct quantity was sent, and nothing was damaged en route. By your standards, it was a perfect transaction, and the fact that the stuff was due to be there last month is a mere detail. They don't agree, and unless you satisfy their buyer, you won't even get the chance to make the same mistake again.

WHAT'S YOUR EXCUSE?

DIVERSION OF BLAME TECHNIQUE

1. I've been tripping out on acid, man.

2. The truck has been impounded by customs.for the last week

3. Our regular lorry driver has won the lottery and left.

SMOKESCREEN TECHNIQUE

1. I've been attending to my wife's funeral.

2. Someone has nicked our forklift truck.

3. Our computer has exploded killing three and injuring one.

DESPERATION TECHNIQUE

1. Our despatch manager has been arrested for exposing himself to minors.

2. They've had a fire at the factory.

3. My wife has run off with the truck. The latest I hear is she's starting her own business.

LAST RESORT

* I only have three weeks to live.

You really want to tell him to sod off, but you can't really do that because the day might come when you actually need to buy some of his wares. The trouble is that at the moment he's as welcome as a fart in a sauna. You have other things to do, like picking a winner in the 2.30.

WHAT'S YOUR EXCUSE?

Diversion of Blame Technique

1. You are a free mason.

2. You are not a free mason.

3. He is in the middle of a crisis.

Smokescreen Technique

1. He is far too busy, if you could wait for a couple of hours.

2. He's in a meeting.

3. He's on a international conference call.

Desperation Technique

1. He has just sold the company.

2. We're going into receivership this week.

3. We're bankrupt, I wouldn't sell him anything at the moment.

Last Resort

* He's making love to Mrs Palm, he won't be long.

Losing an Order

The boss told you it was a sure thing, and that they were desperate. The boss was desperate as well, because he sent you. Not to win the order, but simply to take down the details. You're now outside your own boss's office. He's waiting to find out how much they want. You're having bowel trouble at the thought of telling him that not only do they wish nothing from your firm at all just now, but also they do not wish anything at all from your firm at any time in the future.

WHAT'S YOUR EXCUSE?

DIVERSION OF BLAME TECHNIQUE

1. The competition bribed them.

2. Their buyer was gay.

3. Their boss said you were an asshole so I hit him.

SMOKESCREEN TECHNIQUE

1. I think they are going bust.

2. Their buyer was a mason.

3. Their buyer wasn't a mason.

DESPERATION TECHNIQUE

1. I went to the wrong school.

2. They said our product was shoddy.

3. They wanted a bribe and I has no cash on me.

LAST RESORT

* They wanted 36 months credit.

Caught Sleeping

This is obviously not the time to have to think of an excuse, as the largest part of your mind is probably still thinking up other unspeakable things to do with the women who populate your dreams. You need something thought out in advance to explain your embrace in the arms of Morpheus at such an inopportune time and inappropriate place.

WHAT'S YOUR EXCUSE?

DIVERSION OF BLAME TECHNIQUE

1. I've been in a coma.

2. I fainted.

3. Someone spiked my coffee with angel dust.

SMOKESCREEN TECHNIQUE

1. I've been up sick all night.

2. I've got terrible pains in my chest.

3. Got has been talking to me.

DESPERATION TECHNIQUE

1. I've been overcome with fumes.

2. I was up all night, my daughter is possessed again.

3. I didn't sleep last night. I was repairing the wife's wheelchair.

LAST RESORT

*   I think I've got the early stages of Parkinson's disease.

Caught Stealing

Johnny Cash sang a song about someone who stole a new car from the car factory he worked in "one piece at a time", and it seemed a good idea to you at the time. The firm makes thousands of different components every day and if you can take one, well that's surely not stealing. Let's call it wastage. Tragically the boss isn't likely to agree. Especially as it's just dropped from under your coat.

WHAT'S YOUR EXCUSE?

DIVERSION OF BLAME TECHNIQUE

1. It's not mine.

2. Someone planted it on me.

3. I'm taking it home to test it.

SMOKESCREEN TECHNIQUE

1. I'm making a wheelchair.

2. I'm just borrowing it.

3. I want to see this in daylight.

DESPERATION TECHNIQUE

1. It must have got stuck in my truss.

2. The foreman told me to take it to his house.

3. Please call an ambulance, I think I'm having a heart attack.

LAST RESORT

* God told me to take it.

It was only a pub team wasn't it? It's only for fun and the result doesn't matter. Nevertheless you had invited along your nephew to impress him with your ability. He does look as if an impression has been made on him, the dissaproval on his face is matched only by that which your team mates have been threatening to demonstrate in the dressing room.

WHAT'S YOUR EXCUSE?

Diversion of Blame Technique

1. The referee was the opposition coach's cousin.

2. We couldn't see because of the fog.

3. The opposition were on drugs.

Smokescreen Technique

1. The other side bribed the referee.

2. Our winger called the referee a 'sissy'.

3. The referee was blind in one eye.

Desperation Technique

1. The oranges were drugged at half-time.

2. The ref said if we didn't give him some serious cash we would lose.

3. The opposition's fans were shining mirrors in our eyes.

Last Resort

* Our Centre Half was blind drunk and anyway-it's only a game.

Not Winning at Golf

You heard ten minutes ago that your team was all square in the matchplay back at the clubhouse, and that all you had to do was beat your 14 year old opponent. The walk from the 10th green to the clubhouse will take about 15 minutes, and that's the time you have to decide what you're going to tell your team mates, because you've lost. By 10 and 8.

WHAT'S YOUR EXCUSE?

Diversion of Blame Technique

1. I've been suffering from multiplying eye all morning.

2. I got bitten by a snake when I played that shot out of the rough.

3. My partner was cheating.

Smokescreen Technique

1. Someone has been tampering with my clubs.

2. The greens were too dry.

3. A big girl kept lifting up her jumper every time I putted-and she wasn't wearing a bra!

Desperation Technique

1. My opponent was on drugs.

2. My partner said if I didn't let him win he was going to have my wife and kids murdered by his big cousin.

3. I walked under an electricity pylon and felt dizzy.

Last Resort

* I didn't have my lucky underpants on.

Not Winning a Race

Your offspring looked on with admiration as you lined up at the start of the father's race at the school sports, but the admiration has been replaced by a look of tearful accusation on the part of the aforementioned offspring, and an expression on your wife's face that says "You louse." But you only lost by 30 yards. Mind you, it was the 50 yard dash.

WHAT'S YOUR EXCUSE?

DIVERSION OF BLAME TECHNIQUE

1. I couldn't get my running tights on.

2. Someone shouted at me when I ran past, and it wasn't very nice what they said.

3. Someone has been fiddling with my running shoes.

SMOKESCREEN TECHNIQUE

1. I thought the race was longer so I paced myself incorrectly.

2. Someone was shining a torch in my eyes.

3. I didn't hear the gun go off.

DESPERATION TECHNIQUE

1. One of my opponents gave me a Mogodon

2. Someone put something in my jock strap.

3. God told me not to win.

LAST RESORT

* One of my opponents said if I didn't let him win he would say I made homosexual advances to him in the changing room.

You are probably unique - think of that. You are in all probability the only person in the world who loves your pet. The fact that your pet may regard you as a soft mug has nothing to do with it. You love it, and are quite happy to be amused and fascinated at the indiscriminate nature of its habits regarding eating, excretion, and (let's be polite) mating. What if someone else's amusement and fascination is less than profound?

DIVERSION OF BLAME TECHNIQUE

1. If dogs weren't meant to poo, God wouldn't have given them a bottom.

2. It gives that country smell to the city.

3. He seems to like your leg.

SMOKESCREEN TECHNIQUE

1. He only bit you because you were scared.

2. My dog has as much right to shit on the pavement as the next man.

3. Humping your leg is his way of saying "I like you".

DESPERATION TECHNIQUE

1. He's playing. He only bit you to get noticed.

2. He's just being awkward. He usually does it in our garden.

3. What would bluebottles eat if it wasn't for dogs.

LAST RESORT

*   If you fake an orgasm he'll let you go.

As she pours soft music and warm breath into your ears, you know that this is the moment. "This is the most wonderful thing to happen to me darling" she murmers, just as you are about to reach into your back pocket and pull out your packet of two (it was three but that's another story).She looks bewildered and asks " Do you think I'm diseased or something?" You'd better choose your words carefully, or you've blown your first lay in months.

DIVERSION OF BLAME TECHNIQUE

1. I'm a very considerate kind of chap you know.

2. I'm extremely aware of the dangers of cross infection.

3. I've got to wear a condom. That way I can go on for up to four minutes. Without a condom I'm lucky to last four seconds.

SMOKESCREEN TECHNIQUE

1. I don't want to give you a baby. There is a history of chronic schizophrenia in our family.

2. I can't ejaculate unless I'm wearing a rubber.

3. I don't want you to catch malaria from me.

DESPERATION TECHNIQUE

1. I ejaculate with such force that you would end up with serious internal injuries if I didn't wear this condom.

2. My willy gets so hot at the end, you would get badly burned if I don't cover my penis.

3. The last time I didn't wear a condom the girl had sextuplets.

LAST RESORT

* I must wear a condom since my sperm is radioactive.

Not wearing a condom

Oscar Wilde might have said, "there's only one thing worse than wearing a condom - and that's not wearing a condom".

If your sense of sexual sensory deprivation is greater than your sense of self preservation and social responsibility then you're a pillock. Here are some suggestions for the suicidal psychopath.

WHAT'S YOUR EXCUSE?

Diversion of Blame Technique

1. I can't get one to fit my willy, they always fall off.

2. I'm immune to HIV.

3. I want you to have my baby.

Smokescreen Technique

1. I'm allergic to rubber.

2. The last time I used a condom three of my teeth fell out.

3. Condoms are for sissys.

Desperation Technique

1. I can't get it past my ears.

2. I'm an Mormon.

3. I'm a male chauvnist sexist asshole.

Last Resort

*   I'm not allowed to wear condoms I'm a catholic priest.

Not Getting into Politics

How somebody like you came to be at a classy cocktail party like this must remain a mystery - not only do the other guests inhabit the corridors of power, they probably have the ante - rooms bugged as well. Merging your inferiority complex with the wallpaper is probably the most intelligent course, given that mention of your own job makes eyes glaze with boredom. But when a condescending set of teeth ask why you didn't go into Politics it's time to show that a man has his pride.

DIVERSION OF BLAME TECHNIQUE

1. My great grandfather was a communist.

2. I'm not crooked.

3. I was beaten as a child.

SMOKESCREEN TECHNIQUE

1. I've got false teeth.

2. I've got haemorrhoids.

3. I can't read or write.

DESPERATION TECHNIQUE

1. I love my wife.

2. I believe in democracy.

3. I said the " F " word once when I was a student.

LAST RESORT

* I had sexual intercourse the week before we were married.

Being the nations political quarterback, and calling the play for others is a job for a big man. But when a call comes from a potential candidate asking you to be his running mate you start to doubt his political judgement. As Groucho Marx might have said "You want nothing to do with a Presidency which would have you on the payroll, because you know that you are a Political bozo. Having said that, it's never stopped anyone else. But you don't want to be a heartbeat away from the responsibility. - An outright refusal may offend.

WHAT'S YOUR EXCUSE?

Diversion of Blame Technique

1. I get airsick

2. In a recent IQ test my score was 11. I think I'm probably over qualified

3. I'm honest.

Smokescreen Technique

1. I used to be a female impersonator.

2. One of my arms is shorter than the other.

3. I wasn't in the CIA.

Desperation Technique

1. I am not a clandestine member of the Klu Klux Klan.

2. I wasn't in the Vietnam War.

3. I can't speak Russian.

Last Resort

* I'm an illegal alien.

WHAT'S YOUR EXCUSE?

Here's your chance to see your favourite excuse in print.
This is provided of course that it's funny or cynical or downright daft.
Send it off to us right away the best 100 will be printed in the forthcoming edition.

Please send to:

Lochar Publishing
Attn: Rupert & Chutney McPhail
High Street
Moffat
DG10 9JU
Scotland